Sally's Anthology
Sorrow • Success • Surrender

POETRY BY

Sally Wamaitha

Sally's Anthology of Sorrow • Success • Surrender
by Sally Wamaitha

ISBN 978-1-957497-49-5

First published in the year 2025
Illustrations: Wanji K
Layout: Mantle Vinx
All unsigned images in the layout are AI generated

Dedication

To my family and friends, who have stood by me through every sorrow, success, and moment of surrender. Your presence has been a constant reminder of God's grace, lifting me in my darkest hours and celebrating with me on brighter days. Thank you for being my refuge in times of great distress.

To all who find themselves in moments where facing the next minute feels impossible, may this collection offer solace, hope, and the gentle assurance that we are held in the palm of His hand, no matter where we are.

In these pages, may you find a reflection of your own journey and the courage to embrace each season of life—knowing that we are never alone. Here lie not just words but the very heartbeat of my journey through sorrow, success, and surrender. May this collection remind you that even in the darkest valleys, we are held, we are seen, and we are loved by our Loving God and His people.

CONTENTS

Foreword

After reading much of Sally's work, I still ask myself how she is fully able to capture a range of emotions with a few simple words. It may sound cliché to ask her, "How do you do it?" but I surely know that her life experiences have honed her natural God-given talent, for the written word. We met through Maputo International Church Fellowship and have worked together over a few years. I find myself wanting to have the same clarity with expressing words and emotions.

With every next stanza, I find myself teetering on the edge of an emotional rollercoaster of excitement, heartbreak, and loss. I am in awe of how many simple life lessons you can grasp in each poem. This book shows how therapeutic words can be when they are expressed from the heart; not only the light ones of births and friends but heavy intense emotions like loss of self and others.

I feel like this book is timely, especially in identifying the emotions of loss and how it gets hard to grapple with it. This compilation has work written at different times in Sally's life, it's like reading a symphony of life that helps you understand the woman she has come to be.

Khumbulangu Mhango (Khumbu)
A confidant, cheerleader and church friend

ACKNOWLEDGEMENTS

It is not possible in the space provided to acknowledge all of you who have been, and continue to be, part of my journey.

I would like to thank my Heavenly Father for the gift of life and for allowing me the privilege to record some of my experiences using this genre.

My dear friend and namesake, Anne Mbotela, who is also the editor of this work, for the encouragement to get me writing after some years of dormancy. Thank God for Facebook, where we reconnected early in 2019 when she was advertising a Writers' Workshop, which I enrolled in. The rest is history. She has helped me reignite my writing passion.

Thanks to my sons, Kwambe and Kamau. You know I love you very much and am proud of the gentlemen that you are becoming!

There is not a day or two that I don't thank God for my friend, prayer partner, cheerleader and sister Bongiwe Nsibandze, whom I met in 1995! Even though we live in different countries, we have daily contact. Thank you for your fervent prayers for my family and me.

To my siblings who call me "big sis," thanks for your support, love and laughter!

To all my friends from church, colleagues, past and present, thank you!

Thank you to my talented niece, Wanjiru Kibera, for the creative illustrations of this poetry. You are a gem, and may God continue to increase your talent in the years to come.

Thank you to all who have made these poems come alive

Thank you once again, Anne, through your platform, The Writer's Harbour, for the meticulous work of editing and refining the poems. Thanks for the suggestions you made to make the work presentable.

Endorsements from my sons:

These poems are very personal. They communicate a reality so clearly and so strongly, that you feel like you are visualizing the moment again. This is even within moments that I, as the author's son, have never experienced. It's very beautiful writing!
- Prince

....

Dear Mum,

These poems are deeply moving and personal, capturing emotions and experiences in a way that draws readers directly into each moment. The vivid imagery and raw honesty make every scene feel intensely real, even for events one may not have personally experienced.

The writer's ability to convey such intimate and universal truths makes each piece resonate beautifully, leaving an impression that lingers long after reading. Truly beautiful work, with a unique voice that brings life's challenges and joys into focus in a profound and relatable way

- Kwambe

Introduction

The poems recorded here cover different facets of my life. I talk about different people I have met and how they have impacted my life and provoked different emotions.

Sorrow, Success, and Surrender also encapsulate the truth of God's rescuing hand, no matter what facet you find yourself in. There were times I had no idea how I would deal with the harrowing emotions of loss (for example, the loss of a pregnancy) or my 31-year-old marriage—situations that threatened to take me into a deep hole of doubt. But listening to the soft, still voice of God indicates that he holds each one of us in the palm of his hand. He will never leave nor forsake us. We must be willing to surrender to Him.

God gathers His people from the east, west, north, and south to bring comfort and support in moments of difficulty.

I am learning that in our journey the three components make up our life. The school of life is teaching me to embrace all three and take lessons that will glorify Him.

God bless you and hope this compilation of poems (Anthology) encourages you.

Sally Wamaitha

If I were to grow up again

If I were to grow up again,
I'd live my life to gain—
Not haphazardly,
But instead, quite carefully.

I'd cherish my childhood toys,
And steer clear of distractions and noise.
I'd keep my ribbons,
And treasure my antique clip-ons.

I'd brush my teeth to avoid the drill,
Save my money instead of chasing the thrill.
I'd resist spending on fleeting things,
And invest in what lasting joy brings.

I would not tear books,
But guard them for their looks.
I'd not shove my socks
At my neighbour's block.

I'd recall my manners,
To impress life's planners.
I'd study math to find the way,
And walk the right path every day.

I'd treat history with respect,
Geography I would not neglect.
I'd let photography capture moments,
Instead of chasing fleeting components.

On friends and relations,
I'd weigh all considerations.
With boy-friends and others,
I'd pause, reflect, and not blunder.

But above all, I'd seek a deeper call—
To walk with God through it all.
I'd find strength in faith and love,
And follow His wisdom from above.
In His people, I'd find my place,
Surrounded by His endless grace.

Now that I am grown, I live with the weight
Of choices made, the paths I create.
Yet I thank God, for His mercies are new,
He gives me chances to start fresh and renew.
With each dawn, I'm reminded to strive,
To do life better, to truly thrive.

My violet's delight

She is a violet
Set in the toilet cistern cover
But that, doesn't upset her
Instead, it delights her

All she needs is water
And a little, garden tool
Just to remove the weeds
And help her bring forth new seeds

She also desires light
Not too much of it
For a lot of it
Will make her cry "ouch"

My violet is pretty
And when she's teething
She has purple, soft flowers
Sometimes, she even gets them in pairs

She is my violet
Set on the toilet window;
It doesn't upset her
Instead it delights her.

To my Hero

You're my hero, friend and lover
I would never want another;
For as my thought and so you promise;
To Protect me from malicious individuals

As my friend you never fade
Always like the avocado shade
Giving me your time, your all
What else? I'm in awe!

As my lovely husband
You know my every demand
You know how to request;
As you explore your quest.

How can I thank my hero, friend and lover;
Buy him a token of life's golden wrapper
Just like we need a little sunshine daily
You need a cup to drink up your daily

Written by author in gratitude for a gift my husband gave to me
(a year after we were married, 1990)

When I meet my Mother-In Law

When I meet my mother-in-law
I'll kiss and hug her
The hug will last a minute or two
Because I think it's long, overdue

I'll want to ask her all about her son
From birth, childhood - an active youth
I'll want to laugh and cry with her
Comparing all the photos I've seen of her
And learn about the wonders of a job well-done

I'll try and assure her about my desire
To keep our relationship smooth
That she may also enjoy
The son, she bore and raised up

I'll assure her that as her new daughter;
And when the Almighty God grants His providence
She will be a proud granny
Of offspring, from her beloved son

Sally Wamaitha

Oh, how I'd love to make her happy;
To make her smile, remain on her chubby face
For like sunshine removes the dullness of the day
So, my mother-in law, will replace the loss of my own mother

For my desire is not to have a mother-in-law but a mother-in-love

September 1989, a month after we got married

Sally Wamaitha

You Loved Me Anyway
(Mama Ana)

I remember arriving one hot afternoon!
To your home / your house
You danced, you lifted your tummy!
As you welcomed your daughter
Who you had never met
You smiled, you laughed as you hugged and kissed me
Your hands going smoothly on my face
Telling all who cared to listen, how good it was to see me
You loved me anyway

Our days together were many,
We could not talk to each other!
Whether Bitonga or Portuguese!
How heavy the language sounded to
me I didn't know to seat on the mat
Whether to stretch or fold my legs
But you looked at me smilingly and I knew
You loved me anyway

I came to your house
I didn't know how to prepare the delicacies of your cuisine!
I didn't know how to pound the peanuts,
Or pick the leaves that made the sauces
I didn't know how to scrape the coconut flesh from the hard
shell

And make the liquid to add to the pot
But you loved me anyway

When the babies came and you held them
I didn't know how to make them stop crying
I didn't know how to feed them like you did I didn't know
much, you explained carefully and loved me anyway

I didn't know much, as your daughter
But you loved me anyway,
You prayed for me, you loved your grand children, you loved
us all
Even when I didn't meet your standards!
You loved me anyway

Even in your ailing,
You took your pills
Submitted to drips
You still smiled in your pain
And you loved me anyway

As you breathed your last
You still opened your swollen eyes
Just to say, even in your pain You loved me anyway.
Rest in peace Dear Mama

*Mama Ana passed away on February 1, 2020, 1pm in the presence
of Mana Tininha and Sally*

Sally Wamaitha

Omega, My Other Mother

We met in 1986,
And now it's 2023–
37 years!
Zambia, Kenya, Canada, Mozambique –
The countries that wove us together.
She called me her "Kenyan Daughter"
A title that felt like home.

She cared so much, spoke the
truth, Straightforward, hardworking,
Organized and ambitious, yet gentle.

She loved every living being to bits.

I remember Chocky, her faithful
dog, Resting quietly by her feet,
Welcoming her home after her travels.
Her cats, curling up on her
lap, Purring with each stroke–
Their love reflected her own.

I see her now, walking to the paddocks,
Admiring the cows, sheep, and goats,
The chickens, the ducks, the geese,
All moving in harmony,
As though her presence brought peace.

It was a garden of Eden she created—
Her fields of maize, beans,
And vegetables thriving under her care.

Her orchard, brimming with mangoes, peaches, guavas,
papayas
Tangerines, lemons, and oranges.

I imagine the cows, the goats,
And the sheep felt her love, too.

Her heart was vast,
Sharing itself with all creation.
But then came the interruption.
My other mother—
Diagnosed with cancer.

She never asked, "Why me?"

Instead, she rearranged her life,
As she did with every project she took on.
The chemo, the falling hair,
The nausea and the pain,
The wigs,
The clothes that no longer fit
Her ailing body.

She fought with courage,
Responded to emails, letters, phone calls,
Her strength ebbing and flowing,
Yet she held on.

Victories of remission—brief and hopeful.
I remember seeing her almost recover,
Nourishing herself with healing foods and drinks.
But the cancer returned,
More vicious, more relentless.
It gripped her fragile body,
And life slipped away from her.
I loved my other Mother.
And many others loved her, too.
On her birthday, every year,
October 8, I celebrate her.
She loved life, and now she rests—
In the arms of her Creator.
At 6:45 pm January 31st, 2023 you rested.
But we shall meet again,
In the land of our Creator—another place of connection,
Where time, once more, will bring us together.
I miss you, my Other Mother...

**Sally Kamau (your Kenyan daughter) My dear, other Mother has
since passed away. She was a big part of my life.
Written in 2023**

Every Day is a Miracle

Every Day is a Miracle
I have found that an attitude of gratitude, promotes peace
when there is turbulence
In my more than a century living
I have oscillated from feelings of
apprehension,
anger,
bliss,
courage,
despair,
ego,
fainthearted
gratitude,
happy,
interest,
joy,
knowledgeable,
love,
mad,
numb,
oppressed,
peaceful,
quiet,
restless,
still,
tormented,
unsure,
vigilant,

watchful,
x-hilerated,
yielded,
zealous and then, more...
The Alphabet, doesn't quite cover the feelings I have
revolved around in the years I have been on.
Life's journey!
But I do know for sure, that whether I was in a season of
despair or joy, I can confidently say that GRATITUDE,
remains my single, utmost feeling.

Sally Wamaitha

The Life within me

Makes me rejoice in YOU
For I now understand why
You are the Great Creator

From His to mine, see
You are moulding another being
That you have already planned for
To show your sovereignty

What amazes me Lord,
Is that you choose who to bestow
This gift of parenthood;
Just to show you are God.

Since you have granted us this gift
Give us the wisdom and ability
To bring this being in the way of live
That glorifies you, the Creator

As a future mum, I have my concerns,
Can I bring this life to term?
Or will I have to weep, if it happens
Merciful Lord, may Your Will be done

Oh, dear Lord
Give us the courage to collect;
All the tears of joy or sorrow
If tomorrow comes bright or dark.

The writer lost this pregnancy after 4 weeks

The doctor said it was a missed abortion. This was in September 1991.

Happy Birthday, Son!

A boy was born
My firstborn arrived
An Apgar score of 9/10
A head full of hair!
A loud strong satisfactory cry

On April 8th while the world awaited the release of Nelson
Mandela,
in a pristine hospital in Mbabane
A Dr Stevens, brought you to me
I smiled, no laughed, and cried a little.
You are one of the prayers God answered for me.
He allowed me to be a Mother for the very first time.

So, year after year, whether a party or not, I have
celebrated the day God brought you to me.
Every year!
And today... 30 years ago... I still remember that day.
Not the pain from the stitches, not the cold my body
experienced from the anesthetic effects, but the life I held in
my arms.
YOU!
I kissed your forehead many times.
As you lurched on your food.
You were a baby with appetite
And even today, 30 years later, you still enjoy a good meal.

I know you have lots you could say, or ask, about why we
brought you in to this world.
But for me, the 30 years are a testimony that God has been
carefully choreographing your life.
God has/is still in the business of moulding you into the man
He created you to be.

Yes, there have been some difficult years. Disappointment,
heartbreaks, confusion when things don't make sense...
Yet, you have memories of great times too.

Your 1 de Junho introduction to school, the move to Instituto
Nelia. By the way, the first words you read to me were CO
CA CO LA and I knew my son was no longer illiterate!
Even our two year stay in Australia, you made an impact!
You became the first African school captain. at Amadale
Primary School! What an experience that was!
At Trichardt. you were the overall best student!
UP was your growing space. I know you have great and
tough times to Remember. it's part of life's packages!

In those 30 years, I have smiled, laughed, cried, yelled and
laughed again. I have prayed, fasted begged God for your
success, in your endeavours.
God answers over the years have been
"Yes," "No," "Wait." He answers all the time at His time!
My attitude has been 'may your will be done'. Thank you,
God is good.

30 years cannot be tied in a neat bow. It's been a roller
coaster from day 1 to today! Yet I am still as happy as I was,
on the day I held you;
Minutes after, you were born.

May your years be fulfilling and may your career path be
carved by God, who makes all things beautiful in His time!
May you know that He never forgets that He made you
And has a wonderful plan for you!
I celebrate you Son! Happy Birthday!
Love you! Mum

April 8 1994

*The author was blessed with a baby boy in April 1994 and then
another, on 25 December 1997.*

The Cancer

Trust is precious!
It opens doors for love and understanding
It opens avenues for progress and growth
It opens space for flourishing and blossoming
Trust is precious!

Trust is precious!
Yet, when Trust is eroded by the cancer
Of pride!
Pride cancer cells divide themselves and spread to the heart
They rush to the brain and form tumors
Tumors paralyze the brain's ability, to practice humility
Tumors of pride immobilize the brain's capacity to respond
When Holy Spirit is prompting;
Trust is squashed up, never to be recovered
As the Cancer of Pride spreads

Trust is precious!
But when the cancer of denial permeates down to the
esophagus
It incapacitates the mouth, from acknowledging the truth;
Though it hears Holy Spirit. probing...
The cancerous tumors in the mouth, deny the truth
Eroding trust!
Trust is precious.
Yet, when cancer cells deposit in the lungs
Forming massive tumors;

Breathing becomes labored,
The oxygen gets into the lungs with difficulty;
Depositing tumors filled with sores of mistrust,
Denial, lies, hate, regret, revenge...
Making breathing arduous
Trust needs an oxygen mask!
Because Trust is Precious!

Trust is precious
The oxygen mask,
Helps with the breathing.
But, when the cancer of unforgiveness;
Deposits its cells on the vital organs of the soul
Oxygen is not sufficient.
Nor is Chemotherapy of Prayer;
Neither will the radiation therapy of fasting;
Penetrate the hardened soul.
Except the softened heart
Yielded to the soft voice of Holy Spirit;
Can melt the darkened cells, of unforgiveness
And begin to reconstruct trust
That very Precious Trust

(March 2021)

My Canvas

If I was an artist,
I would sketch bits and pieces of hearts on Canvas
To show the millions of pieces when that heart is broken
I would draw each piece of my heart to tell my story, our
story I would paint them scarlet red, each one of these heart
pieces
And blue for each tear that I have shed
To illustrate the pain that surrounds my broken heart

Each piece of my broken heart
Would carry a tear that has fallen,
As I waited for you to return home
It would carry a prayer I have said to God, asking Him to talk
to you
Each piece of my broken heart
Would carry the words of our wedding vows
One to another

Before God and man
That for better or for worse
In sickness and in health You are my buddy, my buddy, for
life

My Canvas would have a piece of my heart
For Mum (Rest in peace, dear Mama)
For your siblings (departed, Mana Gilda)
For your Dad
For the living ones too!

For nieces and nephews;
Pieces of my heart that I gave to them
Because I vowed, like Ruth, (your people shall be my
people)
Your God, my God

My Canvas would have a piece of my heart
For our handsome sons,
Who will have to call another step-mother;
My canvas will have a piece of my heart
For my lovely grandchildren who will have to
call another, step-grandmother
Or what a canvas of sadness, it will be
Although the colours will be red and blue for tears
It will tell the story of your decisions, your choices!

My Canvas would have a piece of my heart,
To remind me of so many attempts made;
to talk and clear out things that went wrong between us
For all the pleas made
To come clean and sort out our relationship

Of the things that were left unspoken
Perhaps more blue than red, for the tears still flow
My canvas would certainly show, an array of little broken
hearts

Sally Wamaitha

31 Augusts Ago

31 Augusts ago,
I said "I do" to my college sweetheart,
To my dashing prince, so smart and kind,
In the presence of family, friends, and peers,
With butterflies fluttering, nerves intertwined.
I chose laughter over tears,
Happiness over sadness,
Friendship over enmity,
Companionship instead of loneliness,
Joyful adventures together,
Not projects undertaken alone.

31 Augusts ago, I said "I do" to my best friend,
In sickness and in health,
In poverty and in plenty,
Through failures and success,
I vowed to stand by you, come what may.

31 Augusts ago, I said "I do" to have and to hold,
From dawn's first light to twilight's embrace,
Through morning's warmth and evening's glow,
In sunshine's laughter and moonlight's grace.

I said "I do" to love from Monday to Sunday,
From the first of the month to the last,
From January's chill to December's cheer,
I promised, till death do us part—
Only death would sever our bond.

But 31 Augusts ago,
I did NOT say "I do" to walking away,
Nor to treating each other with cruelty.
I did not say "I do" to living apart
When disagreements arose,
Nor to seeking new loves,
Finding new soulmates.
I did not say "I do" to introducing step-parents
While we still walked this earth,
Or to leading separate lives
After declaring our vows.

31 Augusts ago, I said "I do" to you—
A promise strong, meant to endure,
Yet here I stand, alone,
No sweetheart, no best friend,
No soulmate by my side,
And yet, death has not claimed us.

Sadly, there are no more Augusts to celebrate;
The marriage faded into long separation,
And eventually, a divorce—
A chapter closed, yet love remains,
Echoes of vows linger in the silence.

The author was married for 31 years and in this poem reflects there will be no more celebrations for the union.

At the Funeral of my Marriage

Its 10.30 local time
The sky is grey
Motorists hooting and beeping
At traffic lights and at pedestrians
Criss-crossing at illegal pathways
To the irritation of drivers
But on the way to the Funeral of my Marriage

Beside me is an angel, Mercy
She hugs me after bringing me to the Law office
God bless you, Mercy for supporting me
On the way to the Funeral of my Marriage

Am wearing black today
A dress, shiny shoes and handbag
White, pearly looking earrings and necklace
To attend the Funeral of my Marriage

My black handbag
Contains a white face towel
Carefully folded
To soak my tears,
Which flow uncontrollably
How I wish I could press a button on my body
To stop the flow of the tears
that gush out, as the court clerk shuffles her paperwork
At the Funeral of my Marriage

She is professional
Stoic and articulate
"Any chance to resurrect this marriage?'
My gaze shifts to my hubby of 31.7 years
'No chance' comes, the determined response
Enunciating the words as the Law annals
Which expressly dissolves the marriage
I hear in the distance the sound of handfuls of... ash to ash
Dust to dust hit...
The coffin
Containing the remains of 31.7 years of memories

The pens write on the dotted lines
The solemn moment is marked
March 18, 2021, at 11.45 before noon

The law requires her to announce
'You have 8 days to change your mind regarding your
marriage'
After which the 'death certificate' will be produced (my
thoughts)
Out comes my white face towel
Sponging up the river of tears that taint my spectacles
My marriage has been pronounced dead
In attendance, my lawyer, hubby, and court clerk presiding
In the presence of God Almighty
At the Funeral of my Marriage

Outside my angel is waiting
With open arms to support me after the ordeal
She takes me to a quiet restaurant, where we have a
comforting meal
God bless Mercy for supporting me
On the way to the Funeral of my Marriage

My Father God, I know you never desired this for us
You gave us many good years
Two handsome sons
And many other blessings
I will still bless you all the same
Because You deserve praise and honour
Even on the day of the Funeral of my Marriage

DOB 5/5/1989 DOD: 8/3/2021

REST IN PEACE!

Divorced

Dark shades of blue permeate what was Holy matrimony

Indigo twinkles to declare no more Harmony

Violet echoes the bleeding from the soul ventricles causing illness emotionally

Orange illuminates broken walls of the soul affecting each iota of my individuality

Red brings the face of my Saviour, bleeding on a cross to heal these wounds of rejection

Carrying my mistakes, shame and rejection to bring back perfection

Enduring all for the restoration of all those divorced

Dying and resurrecting to restore to the DIVORCED, so that there is no more remorse Even though DIVORCED!

July 2020

Brokenness

It took a climb upon a high bar stool
to retrieve a file, where a travel document was safely stored
The stool tipped and spit me out
Like a brick, I landed on my left arm
It hurt; it was heavy but the pain was excruciating!

My neighbour attended the swelling wrist
With icepacks to keep the swelling down
The pain was unbearable

At the hospital the x-rays confirmed
Piece of bones largely mangled
Lodged inside the flesh of the wrist,
The surgeon pronounced that the bones were in
smithereens!

Repairing the bones
Around the left wrist
Required some hours of surgery
5 hours to be precise
A white huge cast covered the bones in repair

Pain and discomfort resided
On the whole carrying the cast
The cast remaining for 6 weeks!

Friends rallied around me
Driving me to work and home and hospital

Helped with required grooming routines
Supported me as the bones reconnected

I pondered on the broken wrist
My broken marriage
The social distancing implemented by COVID
Everything seemed to be in pieces

But my heavenly Father
Reminded me that He holds all the pieces
And would rebuild me up again
For His honor and glory

So even though the pain was deep
Physically and emotionally
Father God, reminded me
He would repair the broken pieces
And put me altogether again.

April 2020

The accident occurred in her home one evening.
The lesson on God holding the pieces together is profound.

Sally Wamaitha

The Day Before Valentine

I met my Ex
day before Valentines.
I hadn't planned to meet with him
I never make such plans;
For what would I say to him after so many years apart

My Ex needed a document, that I had
For an administrative matter he needed to sort
He had asked for my document
Weeks earlier;

I got it sent to him and thought the matter, settled
He would return it as soon as he completed the task
But lo and behold, he brought it himself;
He was meant to leave it with the security staff at my work-
station

Alas, the security called me;
"Someone is here for you;"
I walked out of my office to meet the visitor
I had no idea who would be coming to see me, so early in
the morning.
There stood, my Ex!
Envelope containing my document, in hand

Seeing my Ex drew a curtain of memories
Of the many Valentines, we had celebrated in past years
The flash back of numerous romantic gestures
The chocolates, red roses, jewelry....
Many coffee dates and dinners....
Phone calls, just to say hello...
And although he believed that Valentine was to be
celebrated with a loved one, daily...
He always did something special for me on Valentines

But today, my Ex was returning my document
There are no more Valentine celebrations with him
Only memories of Valentines with my Ex.

February 2023

Sally Wamaitha

WAMAITHA

Woman created proud and free
Alive and active in life's spree
Manages to smile through thick and thin
Attentive, seeking godly ways
Inquisitive to investigate
Trying to conquer arising, challenges;
Happy to do good, to all she meets
Ah, what a friend, my namesake to me!

Written for my namesake in our University days 1988 – 1992
Who has become my Editor (The Writer's Harbour in Kenya), well
over 3 decades later – There are no coincidences with
God, our good, good, Father.

Sally Wamaitha

Happy Birthday Bongi

Lord I thank you for my friend Bongi Who turns 61 today!
I thank you for giving her to me as a friend I thank you that
you love her so much!
Father, I thank you for Bongiwe Nsibandze, Aka PRISCILLA

Lord, I celebrate my courageous friend and Mother of three
I celebrate her nurturing nature, to Tawanda, Lungi and
Noku.
Lord I celebrate my friend and prayer warrior
Always on bended knee, seeking to serve you every day
Always asking for your direction on how to live each day
Presenting her beloved children, family and friends to you!

Father, I thank you for the wisdom you continue to bestow on
her
As she supports so many who look up to her for
encouragement, inspiration and wisdom
I thank you Father for the resilience she has developed
Because she calls on you for strength to keep going in so
much adversity
How I thank you Lord, for her;
And continue to ask you Father to strengthen my friend
Bongi
Lord I celebrate Bongi's faith
Even when the pantry is bare;
The fuel tank is empty;
The body is ailing,
The bank account is depleted.
She knows you Lord, Jehovah Jireh will provide

She is confident and knows you will heal her as Jehovah
Rapha
And indeed, you have Lord In the most amazing ways
Thank you, Lord for your faithfulness in
her 61 years of life

Lord I thank you for Bongi
I know you will watch over her
As your promise made in Psalm 23
You will be her Shepherd
Thank you, Lord for Bongi
You are a good FATHER to her
I pray that you keep her as Your beautiful bride
Serving and worshipping you
And uphold her in every possible way

Happy birthday Sweet Bongi!
God bless you and shine His face on you every day, in your
new year!

Bongi is my prayer partner. We worked together, for the Australian Govern
ment, between 1995 - 2003

Meet my friend Candi

Let me introduce you to my friend
She wears her long hair loose or in a bun,
She currently has highlights in it,
for that nice contrast touch!
She walks with confidence around her house
Her voice pitch is between soprano and tenor
Her felines, Echo and Sottie, know her voice
So does Gemma her Staffordshire Terrier

Responding to her as she talks to them, like humans
She understands, their moves, their sounds, and feeds them
right on time
They understand her different tones, a cuddle, a reprimand:

They obey her as if to say, "Yes Mum!!" as they sit waiting for
her next instruction!
But they know she loves them all!

Let me introduce you to my friend Candi
Mummy of two; no three!
And recent granny to handsome Mikah
The picture frames decorating the living room Describe the
love she has for her children,
Her siblings, her friends!
My friend Candi, is lovely to be around!
Please meet my friend Candi Engaged to Adrian in April
A fisherman and lover of all sea adventures

His pictures are captured in photos displayed on the walls
around their lounge
And in Candi's face-book wall!

My friend Candi
Has Italian ancestry, South African nationality, and
Mozambican living
She will make you a mouth-watering lasagna:
A cool tasty cheesecake served with black coffee or milk if
you prefer!
A lamb casserole;
Or braai chicken pieces as she makes, creamed baby
spinach.
My friend Candi, talks about the water painting techniques of
Vincent van Gogh Oil paintings of Michelangelo's line
Pastel paintings by Mary Cassatt and others
Acrylic dry brush technics she practices
My friend Candi is passionate about these techniques and
more.
She loves to teach anyone who would like to learn, just give
her a call

My friend Candi loves to teach English, art, cooking
You name it
She would do well in to act as she loves a good dance;
Especially a swirl

My friend Candi, loves Jesus
Each morning, she sends me
"Your Word for today"

Sally Wamaitha

Encouraging me to lean on God for All my needs

My friend Candi, is a just the kind of friend
You and I want to have every day of our lives
I Love you Candi!
God bless you!

Caring for people and cats, that's you!
Adorable, Arty and kind that's you too
Never, gives up; always tries
Determined to reach the skies
Independent and fearless
Dogs you love, Gemma your terrier dearest
Attentive, adorable, admirable: CANDIDA

Thank you for your love, attention, kindness, care! Thank
you for everything!

A Girlfriend who Makes me Laugh

I have a girlfriend who makes me laugh
She belongs to the most noble profession
A teacher!
A mathematics teacher!
Quantitative reasoning to be specific

My girlfriend teaches music
To little kiddies aged 6 to 10!
In addition to classroom adventures my girlfriend tells teens
about God.
She reads from the Bible
Explains the meanings and prays for all

My girlfriend extends her skills to the basketball and volleyball
fields
I think she could play netball too
If asked to.
She mentors the boys and girls
Encourages them to pass on the ball
Allows them to have some adrenaline rush
As part of their growing process

My girlfriend is a Mummy to two male young adults
An Aunty to many nieces and nephews
A granny to a few
And Ms Wilma to many at school, church and afar

Sally Wamaitha

My girlfriend's voice is a high pitched soprano
She helps the teachers and students find the right key for a
song or hymn.
My girlfriend has many talents
And she shares them liberally!

My girlfriend invites me for arty meetings
Where other girls come to draw, paint and doodle
She takes me with to early morning Saturday walks
Where she invites me too breath the fresh morning air
Marvel at the amazing sunrises
As we reflect in the week gone

My girlfriend loves proper coffee
French pressed, or filtered
Not ricoffee granules
That people call coffee!
She loves the Earl Grey Tea
Served in Pretty Dainty cups
With honey to sweeten
And company to relax

My girlfriend loves God
She loves to pray and invites me to kneel before our Father
She is a blessing to me
A girlfriend so special
God bless you Ms Wilma

Blessed Walkers

The blessed walk is a journey of love for Jesus,
binding our hearts with purpose,
encouraging us to rise early on Saturday mornings,
to gather at our chosen spot,
and walk together, step by step, for an hour.

It's not about building muscles or growing stronger,
nor is it about fame or glory,
not about trophies, medals, or recognition
for those who walk each Saturday morning.

The blessed walk is about friendship
rooted in the faith that draws us close;
a shared love and commitment to Jesus,
the author and finisher of our faith.

It's a time to check on one another,
in this walk of life we all tread,
recounting the victories
and failures of our week,
from the places where we make our living.
We end in fellowship—
with a coconut drink, a cup of coffee,
or a simple breakfast, when time and means allow,
supporting each other in every stride.

The blessed walk reaches out to strong women,
in every space where the Lord has placed me;
women who lift and inspire, with hearts open wide,
who walk with grace, compassion, and strength.

The blessed walk extends to every woman,
who reaches out to hold another's hand,
guiding and supporting each other
through the journey of life's winding paths,
walking together, lifting each other's burdens,
as sisters in faith, bound by love and purpose.

It's about encouraging one another as mothers,
sharing the joys and sorrows we carry,
and lifting our children up in prayer.

The blessed walk is all about our love for Jesus,
a bond that strengthens and sustains,
leading us with every step we take,
until we meet again, week after week,
to share in this journey, side by side,
the blessed walk, a testament of faith and grace.

By Sally Wamaitha
October 1, 2024
In celebration and thanksgiving to God, for my walking
sisters who encourage me to be strong despite all the life
challenges! God bless you.

Sally Wamaitha

My pretty smiling Dentist

My pretty, patient dentist
Handles my teeth with utmost care
Her room is painted green
The dental recliner is a mustard-yellow
A dental hygiene tray laden with the tools of the trade

I walk in nervously
Aware of what awaits me
As I glance at the shining instruments
Neatly laid out on the Dentist's action seat
All ready for me, her next patient – Me

My Pretty smiling dentist
Assuredly speaks to me
Inviting me to shed off my handbag and remove my
spectacles
She senses my apprehension
As I look at the shiny instruments
Neatly displayed on her working desk
Following her hand motion
I take a seat at the upright mustard-looking, recliner
While she takes her seat of authority, next to her table of
instruments

She listens intently as I describe my dental nightmare
Nodding with understanding
She assures me that I will feel no pain, maybe just
temporary, discomfort!
She motions me to relax on the recliner

Gently she presses a button on my seat
And down I go
Arriving at an angle where her face and hands
have perfect access to my mouth, the home of my 32 teeth

My pretty smiling dentist,
She places a suction tube on the left side of my mouth
Using a spoon-shaped instrument, begin to prod on my ailing
tooth
Expertly hitting at the damaged surfaces
Drill, suction, drill suction
Until at last satisfaction

My pretty smiling dentist
Reminds me to raise my hand if I feel any pain or discomfort
It feels surreal
Is my dentist welding my tooth?
Why is she spraying my mouth?
Air is also blowing in my mouth!
What is the pretty, smiling Dentist, doing?
No pain, just expected discomfort!

My mouth remains open
She inserts oral swabs now and then
She adjusts the suction tube in my mouth
As my pretty smiling dentist works away
The drill, the water spray, the continuous suction of my saliva

After an hour of lots of drills, sprays and suctions,
Oral swabs are fished out
The suction tube, removed
Am finally allows me to close my
mouth My pretty smiling Dentist
Massages my cheeks,
To relax the muscles that have been in one position

After a mouthwash rinse
My pretty smiling Dentist
Announces, that I'm all fixed
Am ready to leave her room
My next visit is scheduled 6-months from today

My pretty smiling Dentist
Promised me no pain
Only a little discomfort
And she delivered it successfully

I can pay my bill with a smile
And will happily return six months from today
To find my pretty smiling Dentist
who knows how to look after all 32 of my teeth

April 2024

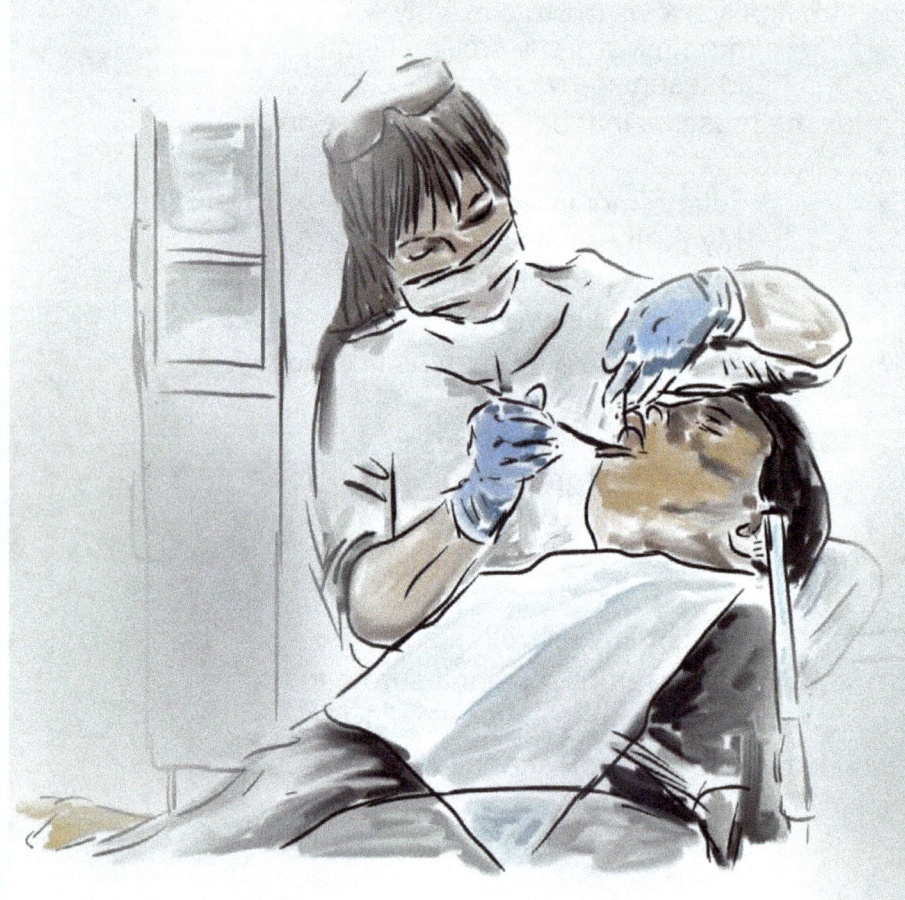

Wanji
24

Sally Wamaitha

How I spent my Saturday!

I spent my Saturday, supervising the repair of
my gate
I don't have the expertise to measure or weld
pieces of iron together;
But the welder required me to be present
He needed me to provide the cool water,
To quench his thirst as he heat-up the metal with
the gas-operated welding machine
The electricity units, needed replenishing
As his machine consumed the units as if to quench its
thirst.

I spent my Saturday with the Plumber
He discovered the leaking pipe, hidden beside the bath tub
The tub had to be dislodged from its original
location until the leaking pipe was fixed;
The plumber's final work required lots of cash,
But finally, we know what caused the wooden tiles to rot.

I spent my Saturday, attending to the carpenter
As he worked to replace the wooden tiles that rot
Due to water infiltration
Water that stealthily crept from a concealed water pipe,
Which leaked due to corrosion caused by age
The escaping liquid, gradually found its home underneath
the wooden tiles,
Causing the tiles to rot
The rotten tiles lifted, as if in protest to the discomfort;
Of the unpleasant water.

The carpenter, peeled them off the cemented floor,
Leaving, rough ugly gaps on the usually level shiny floor
He carried the rotten pieces of tiles out to his working space
To begin the work of salvaging each one

Painstakingly, he worked away;
Assuring me although it is a slow job,
the tiles will be ready to be glued back to the floor
The day came to an end, the work resumes on Monday.
I spent my Saturday
Watching the electrician, rewire the cables in
my kitchen,
Dangling dangerously around the wall
He also replaced the florescent lamps;
Which have been non-functional for a while;
He cleaned up all the light bulbs,
Full of dead curious moths and mosquitoes
I spent the weekend, getting ladders, opening store rooms;
Opening my purse to pay all these labourers;
For all the maintenance jobs done, this Saturday

I meant to spend my Saturday having my car serviced,
For it's in need of a change of engine and break oils,
It's time to change the air and fuel filters;
As they are no longer pleasant to gloss over
But my time was taken by the welder, the
carpenter and the plumber
The Lord-willing, my car will have to wait for another
Saturday.

Sally Wamaitha

As my Saturday ended, I thanked God for giving me a job
and sustenance;
That enables me to do all these maintenance jobs,
That would be otherwise difficult to do,
So even though my Saturday is gone, and the
money depleted,
I know my God will make a way for the other maintenance
jobs
That need to be carried out, with this Saturday, so swiftly done

Sally Wamaitha

SIMBA, "Why don't you Sing, anymore?"

A month ago, I met you -
I was told your name is Simba,
You were named after the king of the jungle!
Because you are the King Cranary at Unit 4, Herries Street,
Newtown
Yellow and bright-bodied!
Visible at the entrance of Unit 4
Why don't you sing anymore?

You are SIMBA because you are strong!
You are majestic! I see how you fly from branch to branch,
In your four-sided fenced, home
When Pam and Dan open the door to Unit 4, it is quiet!
Why don't you sing anymore?

SIMBA: Who upset you?
You surely can arise! You can start to sing again!
Pamela feeds you;
She lets you out to fly around
Daniel, gets you back into your dwelling
Your owners clean your house in Unit 4!
Don't be silent Simba, they keep sighing;
Why don't you sing anymore?

SIMBA, did another bird tell you to forget your voice?
I hear Pamela play happy records of your former tunes;
As if to remind you of the melodies you once sang.
As she wonders,
Why don't you sing anymore?

SIMBA, are you feeling confused,
Like human, teenagers?
Is that why you can't find your tune?
I also wonder why you won't even try, to at least, whisper a
tune
Why don't you sing anymore?

SIMBA, we are in a new year! Its 2024
Forget the past, hurts and challenges
Start the new year with a new tune!
Though I have to say bye-bye
And return to my land;
I hope in 2024
You will sing again.

Sally Wamaitha, while visiting friends in Brisbane, Australia in
December 2023 – January 2024

Wajik
L4

notes

www.ingramcontent.com/pod-product-compliance
Lightning Source LLC
Chambersburg PA
CBHW061710120626
46550CB00003B/1170